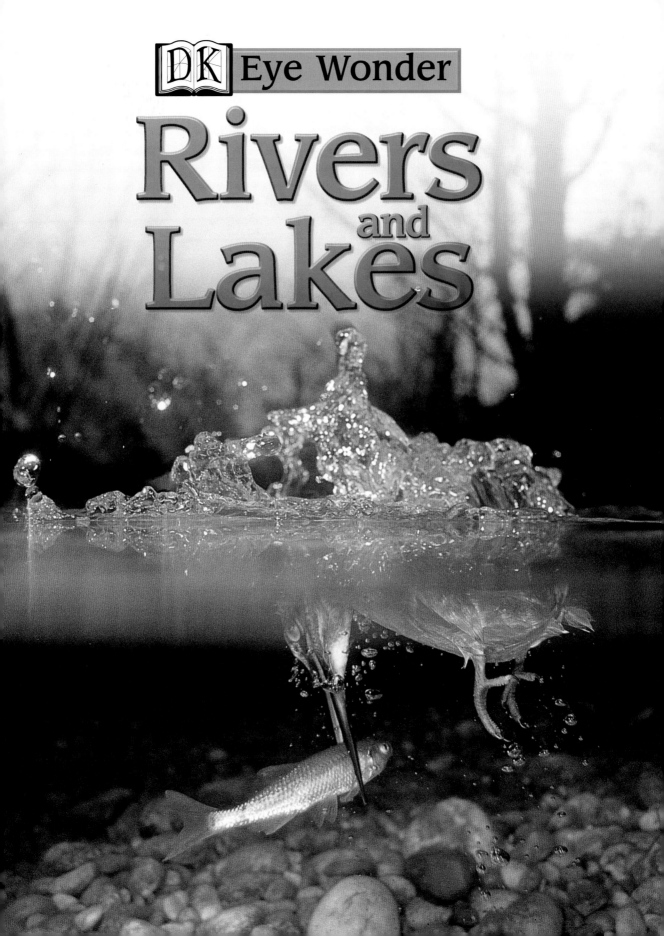

DK Eye Wonder

Rivers and Lakes

LONDON, NEW YORK, MUNICH,
MELBOURNE, and DELHI

Written and edited by Simon Holland
and Anna Lofthouse
Designed by Tory Gordon-Harris,
Mary Sandberg, and Venice Shone

Managing editor Sue Leonard
Managing art editor Cathy Chesson
Category publisher Mary Ling
US editor Christine Heilman
Jacket design Chris Drew
Picture researcher Sean Hunter
Production Shivani Pandey
DTP designer Almudena Díaz
Consultant David Glover

First American Edition, 2003
03 04 05 10 9 8 7 6 5 4 3 2 1

Published in the United States by
DK Publishing, Inc.
375 Hudson Street
New York, New York 10014

Library of Congress Cataloging-in-Publication Data
Holland, Simon
    Rivers and lakes / by Simon Holland and Anna Lofthouse. -- 1st
American ed.
        p. cm. -- (Eye wonder)
Summary: Describes how rivers flow to the sea and the
characteristics of rivers and lakes, including the animal
life found within and near them.
    ISBN 0-7894-9046-3 (PLC) -- ISBN 0-7894-9047-1 (ALB)
    1. Rivers--Juvenile literature. 2. Lakes--Juvenile literature. [1.
Rivers. 2. Lakes. 3. Aquatic animals. 4. Aquatic ecology. 5. Ecology.]
I. Lofthouse, Anna. II. Title. III. Series.
    GB1203.8 .H66 2003
    551.48'3--dc21
                                          2002015141

Color reproduction by Colourscan, Singapore
Printed and bound in Italy by L.E.G.O.

**European
perch**

Contents

Water ways

The world's freshwater is constantly on the move. It flows in and out of lakes, roars down rapids, and runs in rivers to the sea. Its journey never ends.

Great big bathtubs

A lake is a large collection of water that is enclosed by land on all sides. Water from rainfall or melting snow and ice makes its way both overland and underground to fill the lake.

Water that falls as rain, snow, or hail is not salty. This is why it is known as freshwater.

Winding waterchutes

Rivers gather water in much the same way as lakes – but they always have a "source," on high ground, where the flow of water starts.

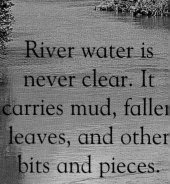

River water is never clear. It carries mud, fallen leaves, and other bits and pieces.

THE WATER CYCLE

3

4

1. Water from the oceans and the ground heats up and rises into the air as vapor.
2. Winds carry the warm, damp air up over higher ground. 3. The water vapor cools and forms clouds. 4. Eventually, raindrops form inside the clouds. Then the water falls back down as rain, hail, or snow. 5. This water makes its way into streams and rivers, either directly, over land, or through the ground. 6. Rivers then carry the water back into the ocean, and the cycle begins again.

2

5

1

6

The Earth's great artist
The flow of water over land slowly wears away the rocks and moves the pieces around. Over time, vast canyons and dramatic valleys have been carved out by moving water.

Source to sea

Rivers have many different stages. Often, they begin as a small spring – an outflow of water from the ground – in a high place. As groundwater and rainwater add to the source, it becomes a stream.

1. Stream-building

Once the source has grown into a stream, one or more streams, or tributaries, may join with it to form a larger, faster-flowing stream.

2. A young river

As more and more tributaries join the main stream, it will soon become a river with a larger "discharge." This means that the speed and amount of water are building up. As the river moves through steeper land, the speed of the flow becomes greater still, resulting in a stage known as "white-water rapids."

River rapids provide ideal conditions for outdoor water sports such as white-water rafting and kayaking.

3. Getting wider

Continuing its journey toward the coast, a river then moves into flatter areas of land. Here, the river slows down, but it becomes wider and deeper, suitable for boats and even large ships.

At this stage, a river will often wind its way through many towns and cities on its way toward the sea.

4. Entering the ocean

Finally, the river approaches its opening into the sea – the estuary, or river "mouth." At this stage it is very broad, and stops looking like a single river. It may split into several smaller, shallow channels cutting through an area of muddy or sandy banks along the coastline.

Black-crowned night herons nest near river and estuary waters.

Frozen solid

Most of the world's freshwater is stored in its frozen form, as ice and snow, in the Earth's polar regions. In cold climates, where the snow never melts, "rivers" of ice called glaciers are formed.

Frozen falls

In bitterly cold weather, waterfalls can freeze solid. The thunderous noise of falling water turns to an eerie silence. Only the "scrunch" of ice picks and spiked boots can be heard, as intrepid climbers scale the frozen water.

Water thoughts

- An "ice jam" can occur when a frozen river thaws out. Large chunks of ice clog up the flow, which causes flooding.

- Glaciers often produce "roaring" sounds that come out of holes called moulins.

White snakes

In places such as the northern US and Canada, the temperature drops so low in winter that rivers freeze solid. Some remain frozen well into the summer months. This frozen river is in Alaska.

Ice diving

Ice diving is practiced by professional divers, who can make money by recovering trucks and snowmobiles that have been trapped in frozen lakes. It is also becoming a popular new sport.

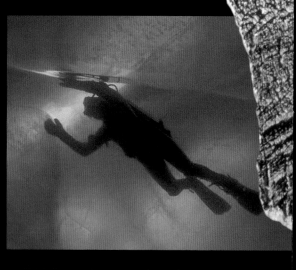

About 10 per cent of the Earth's land is always covered in ice.

Glaciers store about 75 percent of the world's freshwater (in the form of ice).

How a glacier forms

Glaciers often occur in mountainous regions, where a lot of snow falls. Fresh layers of snow push down on the older layers beneath, turning them to ice. Over many years, these thick layers of ice form an icecap. The weight of this ice causes it to creep slowly downhill.

Lonely lumps

As they move downhill, glaciers carry rocky material with them. Huge rocks, known as erratic boulders, often become completely stranded as a result.

Beat the current

Some river creatures have adapted to the challenge of fast-flowing streams or mountain torrents. Sleek bodies prevent them from being swept away or hurled against the rocks by the current.

Deliberately heavy

Just as human divers put weights on to keep them down in the water, caddisfly larvae give themselves extra weight by producing a glue to stick shells, sand grains, or small pieces of stone to their bodies.

Sleek swimmer

The duck-billed platypus has a streamlined body covered in dense, waterproof fur. Its webbed front feet create a bigger "push" against the water, helping this animal to swim faster.

Clever crayfish

Some creatures stay near the bottom of rivers and let the water flow over their backs. Crayfish have smooth shells and sleek bodies that help to resist the current.

The outer shell of a crayfish is hard. Calcium in the water helps to strengthen the shell.

Breathe easy

Trout are at home in cold, bubbly, fast-flowing streams. The bubbles contain a gas called oxygen, which living creatures need to breathe. With this extra oxygen around, the trout can breathe more easily – and so will have enough energy to fight the current.

The steeper the slope, the faster and stronger the water flow.

Water thoughts

● The Atrato River in Colombia, South America, is the world's fastest-flowing river.

● Trout are part of the salmon family. The species (types) found in rivers and lakes include brook, rainbow, and brown trout.

● The marine (sea) lobster is a relative of the freshwater crayfish.

Plenty of room inside!

In spring, a male stickleback's throat and underside turn bright red. This is because he has finished making a nest on the bottom of the river, and wants to attract females to lay their eggs inside it.

Adult sticklebacks only have this reddish tinge to their head and belly when they are breeding (producing young).

Home-makers

Whether it is a nest, a den, or a lodge, river creatures are clever at using plant materials to build their homes – either by the riverbank or in the water.

Builder beavers

Beavers use their jaw muscles and sharp teeth to cut down small trees. Gripping on to the materials, they swim to the construction site to build a sturdy home.

Getting cozy

Minks make dens in riverbank holes, tree hollows, beneath logs, or under tree roots. And just as people snuggle inside their homes during cold weather, minks sleep all day in their dens – especially after snow has fallen.

House-proud

The male stickleback has to build and take care of his nest on his own. The nest has an opening at each end and a soft, hollow pit underneath for storing his eggs.

A stickleback father may clean the eggs using his mouth.

Male sticklebacks fan fresh water over the eggs in the nest using their fins. This ensures that the eggs have enough oxygen.

Cascade

A river falling over a cliff forms a waterfall. Gentle drops over rocky steps are cascades, while larger amounts of water are cataracts The noise and spray of plunging rivers creat amazing natural wonders of the world.

Awesome Angel Falls

In 1933, James Angel found a waterfall in Venezuela – the highest in the world. It is two and a half times taller than the Empire State Building in New York City.

Widest water veil

On the border of Zimbabwe and Zambia, in southern Africa, the Zambezi River flows to the brink of a dramatic gorge. Here, it crashes down to create the widest sheet of falling water in the world.

Plucky ducks

Torrent ducks are quite fearless. They stand at the bottom of small waterfalls to feed. They like to eat stonefly larvae.

These torrent ducks, from the Andes mountains in South America, spend their whole lives in fast-flowing mountain streams.

14

Watery stairs
Watching waterfalls is
fascinating, as the direction
of the stream turns one way
and then the other. This Irish
cascade eventually falls into
the Lakes of Killarney.

A rock pool

15

Feeding frenzy

We humans often eat with a knife and fork, but many river creatures have much more inventive ways of feeding. Some dig, some grab – while others spit or even stab!

"Gotcha!"

Caught! Herons have good eyesight, which they use to scan the water for any signs of life. If a fish comes within striking range, the heron leans forward – partly extending its neck – and then suddenly lashes out with its bill to stab the prey.

Picnickers

Water voles often take their food to places near the water's edge to eat. They like to feed on tasty green leaves and sometimes leave chewed stems behind.

Frog arrest

A giant water bug is able to capture large creatures using its clawed front feet. It can also inject chemicals into the prey. This poison turns the prey's insides into liquid, which the water bug can then suck up as food.

Water arrows

Archerfish are famous for spitting jets of
water at insects above the water. This causes the
insects to drop into the water, where they become
a tasty snack. If an archerfish is very hungry,
it can leap out of the water to catch a fat fly.

*This archerfish
is shooting a fine
stream of water
droplets from
its mouth.*

Dippers and divers

Many creatures live both in and out of freshwater, and some – such as the spectacula kingfisher – have developed eye-catching ways of entering the water. Others are always dipping their heads under the surface to see what is on the menu.

Plunge diver

A quick flash of brilliant blue – that is the sight of a kingfisher diving for any small fish it can grab with its sharp bill. Before diving, a kingfisher hovers over the water, or watches from a branch, ready to strike.

Silvery minnow

The kingfisher never uses its bill to spear prey. Instead, it grabs the fish and kills them out of water.

BREATHING SPACE

Unlike human divers, the great diving beetle has no need to use any scuba-diving equipment for breathing underwater. Diving beetles can gather together a supply of air by trapping it under their wings while they are at the surface, before taking it down into the water with them.

Olympic legs

Most types of frogs have long back legs that enable them to take long leaps. They also have webbed feet, which push against the water like a diver's flippers. This means they are good swimmers, as well as impressive jumpers.

18

Table manners
Ducks like showing off their bottoms, even at dinnertime. This is because one of the ways they find food is by looking just below the surface.

Frogs come to the surface to take in air. They can also breathe through their skin.

A dinner in dipper land
Dippers are able to feed underwater as soon as they are old enough to leave the nest. These fearless birds wait on boulders, and then dive into a white torrent of fast-flowing water in search of food.

Dippers can "walk" underwater.

Wiggly rivers

All rivers "meander," which means that they swing from side to side. Rivers only flow in a straight line if people have built concrete banks on either side.

The river changes direction but remains at a similar width.

A river snake

The river twists and turns, forming a snakelike shape, as it reaches flatter land – the middle part of its journey. The water flows fastest around the outside of the bend, and slower on the inside.

Faster-flowing water travels around the outside of a meander (river bend).

Beaches are formed on the inside bank of some meanders as the water slows down and drops its load of silt and mud.

Oxbow lakes

An oxbow is formed when a meander gets bigger and bigger, creating a narrow-necked loop. Due to flooding and erosion, the oxbow loop can get cut off completely and left as a separate lake by the side of the river.

Small but deadly – these red piranhas, found in South American rivers, have razor-sharp teeth.

V-shaped valleys

Some hill valleys overlap each other, forming a crisscross pattern. This means that a river has to bend and twist in and around the curves of the land.

Bankside living

Tapirs, crocodiles, and capybaras all like being near tropical rivers. Each animal has its sense organs (eyes, ears, and nose) high on its head so that it can keep out of trouble when swimming.

Big river dwellers

Although they are not as wide or as deep as the oceans, rivers are home to some big animals. These river creatures have specially adapted bodies for life in the water, such as webbed feet and waterproof fur.

Otter Olympics

Sleek and streamlined – river otters like to play chasing and diving games in the water. Their outer coats are waterproof, and their long, muscular tails help them to swim.

Otters close their nostrils and ears when swimming, to stop the water from getting in.

A river rodent

The coypu is one of the world's largest rodents. Its short, rounded ears and small eyes – set high on its head – are used to sense any dangers when in water. Coypu families live in bankside tunnels.

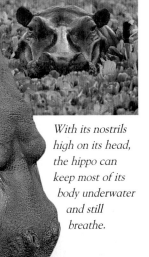

Hefty hippos

Hippos weigh up to 10,000 lb (4,500 kg). With a bulky body and short legs, hippos can move surprisingly gracefully when swimming, walking underwater, or trotting on land. They graze on grass at night and laze in the water during the day.

With its nostrils high on its head, the hippo can keep most of its body underwater and still breathe.

Bloated floaters

West Indian manatees munch their way through lots and lots of water plants. They can stay afloat with ease, even though they are enormous mammals. As they digest the plants, they produce lots of gas, which adds to their buoyancy (ability to float).

A manatee uses its flippers for swimming and for pushing food into its mouth.

Water thoughts

● Manatees can remain under the water for up to 20 minutes before rising to the surface to breathe.

● Hippos search for food on land at night and have been known to eat sugarcane and corn.

● Otter cubs learn to swim just three months after they are born.

About lakes

A lake is a big area of water, enclosed by land. Lakes form when water flows into a hollow or crater faster than it can escape. Melting ice and snow on mountain tops, for example, feed lakes in the valleys below.

Lakes in craters

Exploded volcanoes leave holes, called craters, behind. If the base of an inactive volcano's crater is solid, the water cannot escape. As a result, lots of water collects and a crater lake is formed.

All types...

A crystal-clear lake nestled at the bottom of a mountain looks beautiful, but not all lakes are like this. Earth has a tremendous variety, from small fish ponds to the largest freshwater lake of all – Lake Superior, in North America.

40 percent of the world's total lake water is in Lake Baikal, Russia

Dragonflies are racing champions that can fly at speeds of up to 60 mph (95 km/h).

The Great Lakes

Superior, Michigan, Huron, Erie, and Ontario, plus their connecting channels, form the largest area of freshwater on the surface of planet Earth. These five enormous lakes are visible from the Moon.

Man-made lakes

A reservoir is a man-made lake that is formed when a dam is built on a river. The river water backs up behind the dam to create the reservoir.

A water bird called a reed warbler weaves its nest around plant stalks.

Cattails have distinctive brown "pokers" full of thousands of seeds.

and the Great Lakes of North America.

Life on a lake

Lake life involves a host of submerged (underwater) plant and animal species, but it is important to remember that there is also a lot going on at the surface.

Built to travel

Water boatmen are talented movers. They use their oarlike back legs to "row" across the surface of a pond. Thanks to their wings, they can also leap out of the water and fly away.

Alert! Alert!

The highly sensitive eyes and whiskers of this giant otter can detect very tiny movements in the water. This helps the otter to capture the prey on which it feeds, such as fish and crabs.

Giant otters can grow to 4.6 ft (1.4 m) in length, which is about the height of a child.

Plant platforms

Giant water lilies, in the Amazon region of South America, can measure up to 4 ft (1.2 m) across and are strong enough to hold a small child. Floating plants, such as water lilies, benefit from receiving a lot of sunlight, which they use to make their food.

Walking on water

The wattled jacana bird is also known as the "lily-trotter." It has extremely long toes, which spread out its weight so that it can run along floating plants or the surface of the water.

Floating water plants make great homes for birds, mollusks, worms, spiders, and crustaceans.

Giant water hyacinths

Male jacanas build the nest, while the females, which are much bigger, defend it from predators.

Jacanas build their nests on floating vegetation.

27

What lurks in lakes

The deeper parts of a lake, down to the very bottom, receive less and less light. In these darker and murkier waters, creatures can hide away and surprise their prey.

Pike bites

A pike lies in wait, well-hidden, or camouflaged, among brown waterweeds. The pike remains very still, then bursts out to snap up passing fish, or any other meaty meals.

Sideways sensing

This frog has sense organs along its sides. The organs detect tiny vibrations in the water that help it to find food and avoid predators in the murky waters at the bottom of lakes and ponds.

African clawed frog

A LURKING LEGEND

As legend has it, a lake in Scotland is home to a creature called the Loch Ness Monster – or "Nessie" for short. People claim to have seen a huge hump with a long, giraffelike neck casting a dark shadow on the surface of the lake. Those eager to prove the existence of the monster have used all sorts of technology to try to find it.

Puppy power

A mud puppy has a flattened, eel-like body so that it can burrow (dig) under rocks and logs. It also has feathery red gills that make it look like it is wearing a long red scarf!

Dragonfly nymph

Dragonfly nymphs hatch out of eggs laid in water. These young dragonflies are the same color as the bottom of the pond or lake. This helps to hide them from predators.

Nervous newts

Newts are shy creatures that hide in damp places or underwater. They have slimy skin, a long tail, and a rounded head. Some walk over the muddy bottoms of ponds using just the tips of their fingers and toes – similar to a person creeping around on tiptoe.

These newt tadpoles are only a few weeks old.

29

Swampy wetlands

Muddy coastlines, where rivers approach the sea, are sometimes edged with swamps, marshes, and mangrove forests in tropical parts of the world. Salty water washes in and out of these areas as the tides come and go.

Swamp snakes

The poisonous cottonmouth snake lives in swamps, bayous, and slow-moving rivers in the southeastern US. It got this name because of its pure white mouth, which can be seen each time the snake displays its fangs.

Low tide tidbits

Fiddler crabs cannot feed underwater. They have to wait until low tide, when they emerge from their burrows to pick small bits of food from the mud.

Mudskippers have strong front fins and a special sucker on their belly to help them climb up and cling on.

Fish out of water

As the tide comes in, mudskippers climb up mangrove roots and branches to avoid predators. When the tide is out, they plop down onto the mangrove floor to feed on creatures living in the mudflats.

The mangrove floor is covered in prop roots, which are easier to see when the tide is out.

A tangled mess

The trees in a mangrove forest have roots that grow into the air instead of down into the soil! These "aerial roots" allow the tree to breathe in the salty water. Meanwhile, "prop roots" hang down into the mud to give the tree extra support.

The mouth

An estuary, or river "mouth," is where the river's freshwater flow finally comes to the end of its journey and runs into the ocean. This part of a river is a mixture of land and sea, and of freshwater and saltwater.

Half river, half sea...
River estuaries are affected by the tides of the sea, but are protected from waves, winds, and storms by the surrounding banks of sand, land, and mud.

Chisel-beaks

Oystercatchers feed on mussels, limpets, and cockles. They get into the shells by chopping the muscle that holds the shell halves together, or by bashing them open against rocks or sand.

Search and destroy

Avocets find food in the wet mud. They sweep their long, curved bill to and fro in search of small worms and shrimp.

Pied avocet

Mudflats are as useful to a wading bird as refrigerators and pantries are to human beings.

Mudflats

As a river nears the sea, where the land is flatter, it slows down and dumps its load of mud and sediment. This creates huge areas of mud where flocks of birds come to feed.

THE THINKER

Herons are quite intelligent when it comes to catching fish. The black heron spreads its wings to cast a shadow on the water. This attracts groups of fish, because they like to bask in the shade. The heron then grabs them with a quick thrust of its bill. Like fishermen, some even use bait to lure their catch.

Hermit crab

Taking shell-ter

Estuary-dwelling creatures, such as shellfish, find protection from birds and other predators at high tide. For extra safety, some only hunt at night.

Purple crab

Salmon marathon

Traveling is an important part of a salmon's life. Born upstream in rivers, the young salmon migrates (travels a long way) to the ocean to feed and grow. When ready to spawn (lay eggs) it swims thousands of miles back to the river where it first hatched.

People fish for the large adult salmon as the fish return to the streams where they were born.

1. To the river

Once they have reached their destination, the female sockeye salmon dig a nest in the gravelly river bed – where they lay up to 4,300 bright pink eggs, which the males then fertilize.

2. To the lake

As soon as the sockeye salmon fry (baby salmon) hatch and emerge from their gravel nest, they make their way toward the nearest lake.

When they set off for the freshwater lake, salmon fry are only about 4.3 in (11 cm) long at the most.

The powerful jaws and paws of

3. To the sea

After spending about a year in a freshwater lake, the sockeye salmon journey to the saltwater ocean, where they will remain for most of their lives. At this time, they have blue-gray heads and backs, and silvery sides.

Brown bears try to grab the spawning salmon as they leap above the surface during their journey upstream.

34

4. The final lap

About four years into their lives, the adult salmon return to their home streams to breed, sometimes traveling as far as 930 miles (1,500 km). After spawning, they die.

the brown bear are a danger to salmon.

Water thoughts

● When the sockeye salmon leave the ocean, their bodies turn from silver to bright red.

● A salmon's strength can be defeated by turbines and sluiceways in river dams.

● Sockeye salmon live in the US, Japan, the Canadian Arctic, and Siberia.

Stop the flow

People build dams to restrict and control the flow of water in a river. Throughout history, dams have been used to prevent flooding and to irrigate (water) farmland. Today they are also used to produce electricity.

Giant cork

The Glen Canyon Dam, in Arizona, is 710 ft (216 m) tall and 300 ft (91 m) thick at the bottom. The restriction of the water causes an artificial lake (a reservoir), called Lake Powell, to build up behind the dam.

Once the dam was built, it took 17 years for Lake Powell to completely fill up behind the barrier.

This is the Glen Canyon Bridge.

Detour ahead

Often, a river has to be diverted (moved elsewhere) while a dam is being built. Builders took three years to carve a new channel for the Paraná River, in Brazil and Paraguay, so that they could construct the Itaipu Dam.

The Thames Barrier in London, England, is the largest flood barrier (with movable gates) in the world.

Flood barriers

Movable flood barriers have gates that can be closed to stop river waters from flooding certain areas, such as towns and cities, at high tide.

Hydroelectric power

Many dams are used to generate electrical power. In some countries, nearly all electrical energy is supplied in this way.

The dam contains large motors called turbines. Huge amounts of water are released through the barrier, into the river below, making the turbines spin. The spinning turbines drive generators to produce electrical power.

37

Flooded

Whether it is due to a sudden downpour of heavy rainfall or a long period of very wet weather, too much rain can cause rivers to flood. Flooding can cause serious problems for people, animals, and the land nearby.

Here comes the rain...

In periods of heavy rainfall, the ground gets completely soaked with water. This forces lots of rainfall to flow overground – directly into rivers and streams, which may then overflow.

A flash flood

Some floods happen without warning, often after a thunderstorm. In steep, narrow valleys and gorges, there is nowhere for the water to go, so it gushes downhill – very quickly.

Evacuation

Sometimes cities, towns, and villages are so badly hit by flooding that people have to be evacuated (taken away) from the area. The risk of landslides, drowning, and diseases means that it is simply too dangerous to stay there. Trained rescue workers help people to get away safely.

Defenses

In areas where floods regularly occur, engineers work on ways to prevent rivers from bursting their banks. Sandbag barriers are only a temporary defense, so rivers often need to be adapted so that they can hold the extra water.

Dried out

A long period of dry weather, with much less rainfall than usual for the time of year (or none at all), is called a drought. During a drought, rivers, streams, lakes, and ponds carry much less water – and they can even dry up completely.

Where the water goes...

The water in rivers and lakes gets heated up by the Sun, and rises up into the atmosphere as water vapor. This is called evaporation. When there is not enough rainfall to replace this lost water, rivers and lakes can dry out very easily.

A dried-out lake in Thailand (above)

Farmers in hot climates often rely on regular floods to bring water and nutrients to the soil and boost plant growth.

Periods of little rainfall mean that aquifers may not refill, causing village wells to dry up.

How wells work

Wells, dug into the earth, get their water from underground rock clusters called "aquifers," which store rainwater that has soaked deep into the ground.

Trapped

It looks as if somebody has carved an intricate pattern into the mud at the bottom of this drying lake in Tanzania. These shapes are in fact caused by the bodies of catfish that have become trapped by the shortage of water.

Crop damage

All plants need water to make their own food for growth and survival, so drought is bad news for farmers. Their communities depend on healthy crops.

Polluted

Imagine living somewhere that is always dirty. Sadly, this is the case for some wildlife as a result of pollution in rivers and lakes. River cleanup projects around the world are helping to improve this situation.

Polluted wastewater is being pumped out of a mine through this pipe – poisoning a freshwater river.

Waste-colored waters

Rivers are often polluted by liquid waste products from factories, or pest control treatments used on farms. Very strict laws have been passed to try to make sure that industries deal with their waste properly.

Hard to breathe

Waste from boats and industries located in river estuaries can have a serious effect on wildlife. Oil can spill from boat engines or tankers, and this blocks the supply of oxygen to fish.

Factories are often built close to rivers, which can be used as a water supply.

"Lime drops"

In Scandinavia, many lakes are very clear – but this is actually the result of acid rain pollution, which reduces the amount of life in the lakes. This helicopter is dropping lime into a lake, to cancel out the life-killing acid.

Going with the flow

This woman in Nepal is washing her dishes in river water, but this may not be entirely safe. Upstream, the river is polluted. The dirty water can flow a long way, affecting both people and animals farther downstream.

Out of the ordinary

They may just be pits in the ground full of water, or snaking, watery chutes on their way to the sea – but lakes and rivers can be highly impressive in their size, appearance, and what they contain.

The amazing Amazon

The mighty Amazon River, in South America, carries more water than any other river in the world – enough flow to fill one million bathtubs in less than a minute.

Dead salty

Not all lakes are freshwater lakes. There is a lake between Israel and Jordan named the "Dead Sea," because it contains too much salt for fish to live in it. Its high salt content makes it very easy to stay afloat while swimming in it.

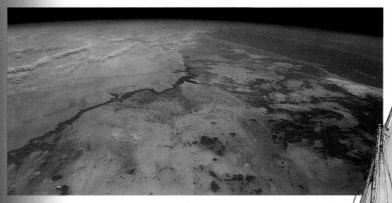

"Felucca" boats have been around for centuries, and are still the main form of transport on the Nile today.

The never-ending Nile

The River Nile is made up of two rivers, the White Nile and the (smaller) Blue Nile, which combine to form the longest river on the planet. It measures 4,132 miles (6,648 km) long from source to sea.

The Mastigias jellies in Jellyfish Lake contain special cells that allow them to produce their own food simply by basking in sunlight.

Jellyfish Lake

Millions of years ago, changes in the land created a lake – in Palau, Micronesia – that is now completely cut off from the sea. The lake still contains a variety of jellyfish that once only lived in the ocean.

Divers can swim among the stingless jellies of Jellyfish Lake in total safety.

Water thoughts

● Over time, the *Mastigias* jellyfish in Jellyfish Lake have lost their ability to sting, while the same species in the nearby ocean can still inflict a nasty bite.

● The Amazon River collects water from a region more than 10 times the size of France.

Glossary

This A-Z glossary explains important words to do with rivers and lakes.

Acid rain water in rain, hail, or snow that is polluted as a result of certain chemicals and waste products being released into the atmosphere.

Aquifer a rock formation, underground, that is capable of holding large amounts of water. Aquifers provide water for wells.

Atmosphere the layer of gases that make up air around the Earth. The air includes the gases that plants and animals need to breathe.

Bayou a boggy, marshy area beside a lake or river.

Billabong this word, mainly used in Australia, is another name for an oxbow lake.

Buoyancy the ability of some objects and living creatures – such as aquatic birds – to float on the surface of water.

Camouflage the way animals hide themselves by blending in with their natural surroundings – often using the shape and color of their body parts.

Cascade a small waterfall. A gentle flow of water dropping down over rocky steps of land.

Cataract a waterfall, bigger than a cascade, where a large amount of water gushes over a rocky drop.

Climate the climate of a certain region describes the type of weather it usually has over one whole year. For example, a mountain climate usually has a great deal of snow, rain, and cold weather for much of the year.

Crater a bowl-like hollow, or depression, that has formed in the landscape – for example, at the top of an inactive volcano. Over time, "crater lakes" can form as water gradually fills these hollows.

Current a "path" of water, within a river or lake, that flows in a certain direction.

Dam a bank, wall, or barrier built to block the flow of water in a stream or river.

Discharge the measurement of the size and speed of a river's flow

Drought a long period of dry weather, during which an area receives much less rainfall than usual for the time of year.

Erosion when rock or soil is loosened and carried off by glaciers, rivers, winds, and waves.

Estuary the wide mouth of a river, where its freshwater meets the salty tidal waters of the sea.

Evaporation the process through which liquid water heats up and changes into water vapor (a gas), which rises into the atmosphere.

Fertilization the step in the reproduction of living things that takes place when cells from a male and female combine – for example, when a sperm fertilizes an egg.

Freshwater the water from rain,

hail, and snow that flows in streams and rivers and is not salty.

Gills the special organs that aquatic (water-dwelling) creatures, such as fish, use for breathing (taking in oxygen) underwater.

Glacier a huge collection of ice, added to by snow in mountainous areas. Glaciers slowly creep downhill, where they either melt or break up into icebergs.

Gorge a deep, narrow, steep-sided area of land through which rivers usually flow.

Icecaps the permanent coverings of ice found in the Earth's polar regions and on mountaintops in cold climates.

Irrigation the adding of extra water to plants and farmland, often using freshwater from rivers and reservoirs.

Larva an early stage in the life of some animals, after birth or hatching, when the young animal looks very different from a fullydeveloped adult.

Loch this Scottish word is another name for a lake, or a large area of seawater enclosed by land (but not on all sides).

Meander the name for a gentle curve or sharp bend in the course of a river (in its middle stages).

Migration the name for the way animals travel long distances to a new home at certain times of the year, or at certain stages of their life – often in large groups.

Oxbow lake a cut-off loop of water, formed when a river meander gets so big – and the water wears away at the land so much – that it becomes a separate lake beside the main river course.

Oxygen a gas contained in the atmosphere that is breathed in, or absorbed, by almost all living creatures to release energy from food.

Pollution damage to the environment caused by chemical dumping or dirty waste products.

Precipitation the general name for the freshwater that falls from clouds as rain, hail, or snow.

Predator an animal that hunts and eats other animals (its prey).

Prey an animal that is hunted and eaten by other animals (its predators).

Reservoir an artificial (man-made) lake used to store water for purposes such as irrigation.

Saltwater the water in the seas and oceans that has salt and other minerals dissolved into it. The salt and minerals mainly wash into the sea from the land.

Sediment small pieces of solid material that get dragged along with the flow of the river water, and then settle to the river bed when the flow slows down.

Spawning the process by which certain animals produce a mass of eggs, and lay them in water, to breed (have babies).

Tadpole the name for the larva (young stage) of a frog or toad.

Tributary a stream that runs into another to form a larger stream with a greater discharge.

Valley a lowland area between hills or mountains. Rivers flow through valleys, and are fed by the precipitation that moves down from the higher ground.

Water cycle the process during which water heats up, rises into the atmosphere, forms clouds, falls as precipitation, and then returns to the ocean via rivers.

Water vapor water in the form of a gas, after it has evaporated.

White-water rapids the fast-flowing part of a river that flows through steep, rocky land, causing the water to foam. This foaming makes the water appear white.

Index

Crested newt tadpole

Acknowledgments

Dorling Kindersley would like to thank the following people for their help in making this book: Venice Shone for original artwork illustrations; Sarah Mills and Gemma Woodward for DK Picture Library research; Abbie Collinson and Sonia Whillock for design assistance.

Picture credits

The publisher would like to thank the following for their kind permission to reproduce their photographs: a=above; c=center; b=below; l=left; r=right; t=top

Bruce Coleman Ltd.: Erwin & Peggy Bauer 13cl; Jane Burton 16clb, 28bc; Jules Cowan 5br; Gerald S. Cubitt 4-5; Paolo Fioratti 1; Jeff Foott 34c, 34clb, 34cb; Sven Halling 22-23b; Joe McDonald 30cl; Dr. Eckart Pott 35b; Marie Read 27b; Hans Reinhard 22c; Tom Schandy 33tr, 47tr; Kim Taylor 17c, 48c. **Corbis:** Yann Arthus-Bertrand 32; Richard Gross 37b; James Marshall 14tl; Buddy Mays 36; Stephanie Maze 43tc; David Muench 9br; Jeffrey L. Rotman 45; Sygma/Allen Martin 38cl; Patrick Ward 14cr. **Joe Cornish:** 15. **Getty Images:** Cousteau Society 8br; Pascal Crapet 8cra; Cameron Davidson 20ac; Terry Donnelly 21cl; Howie Garber 6l; Chris Noble 8l; Richard Passmore 44tr; Manoj Shah 22cb; Grant Symon 4tl, 4cla, 4tll;

Robert Van Der Hilst 9. **ImageState:** AGE Fotostock 37tr; Alan Blair 6r. **Katz Pictures:** FSP/Gamma 39, 40-41b. **FLPA – Images of Nature:** E. & D. Hosking 14bl. **NASA:** 44bl. **Natural History Museum:** 23r. **N.H.P.A.:** Daniel Heuclin 31br; Dave Watts 10cra; David Woodfall 7r; GI Bernard 17br; Kevin Schafer 26c; Lutra 11c; Stephen Dalton 16cr, 22cb; T. Kitchin & V. Hurst 35t; Tom and Therisa Stack 23cl. **Oxford Scientific Films:** 17br, 28c; Paulo De Oliveira 2l, 3r, 48l, 48r; Professor Jack Dermid 17tr, 29cla; Max Gibbs 2bc, 3cb, 3br; Joan/Root/SAL 41tl; Chris Knights/SAL 33cla; Victoria McCormick/ AA 34bc; John Mitchell 16br; Michael Pitts 21tc; Edward Parker 27tl; Andrew Plumptre 22tr; F. Polking/ OKAPIA 16tl; Herb Segars/AA 23; Tom Ulrich 13tr. **Pa Photos:** EPA 38br. **Science Photo Library:** Worldsat International 23tl; Still Pictures: 40tr; Andre Bartschi 44cl; Gilles Corniere 42tr; Glen Christian 41tr; Mark Edwards 43cra; Reinhard Janke 42cl; Yves Lefevre 31; Max Milligan 7l; Tim Rice 33cr, 46l, 47r; Hartmut Schwarzbach 42-43b. **Warren Photographic:** 20-21. **Jerry Young:** 21b.

Jacket credits – Bruce Coleman Ltd.: Jane Burton front br; Dr. Eckart Pott front bl. **Getty Images:** Doug Armand front bc; Cameron Davidson front t; Rick Rusing back.

All other images © Dorling Kindersley. For further information see: www.dkimages.com